U.S. MARSHALS

BY ABBY COLICH

CAPSTONE PRESS

a capstone imprint

Blazers Books are published by Capstone Press,
1710 Roe Crest Drive, North Mankato, Minnesota 56003
www.mycapstone.com

Library of Congress Cataloging-in-Publication Data
Names: Colich, Abby, author.
Title: U.S. Marshals / by Abby Colich.
Description: North Mankato, Minnesota : Capstone Press, [2018] |
Series: Blazers. U.S. federal agents | Includes bibliographical references
    and index.
Identifiers: LCCN 2017039235 (print) | LCCN 2017047997 (ebook) |
    ISBN 9781543501445 (eBook PDF) | ISBN 9781543501407 (hardcover)
Subjects: LCSH: United States. Marshals Service—Juvenile literature. |
    United States marshals—Juvenile literature. | Law enforcement—United
    States—Juvenile literature.
Classification: LCC HV8144.M37 (ebook) | LCC HV8144.M37 C65 2018 (print) |
    DDC 363.28/20973—dc23
LC record available at https://lccn.loc.gov/2017039235

Editorial Credits
Nikki Bruno Clapper, editor; Kyle Grenz, designer; Svetlana Zhurkin, media
researcher; Katy LaVigne, production specialist

Photo Credits
AP Photo: South Florida Sun-Sentinel/Susan Stocker, 19; Dreamstime:
Photographerlondon, 10–11; Getty Images: Scott Olson, 28–29; iStockphoto:
FatCamera, 9; Newscom: MCT/Chuck Liddy, 16, Reuters/Jonathan Ernst,
22; Shutterstock: Felix Mizioznikov, cover (front), franz12, 27, Lee Snider
Photo Images, 23, Leonard Zhukovsky, 18, Noel Powell, cover (top right),
wavebreakmedia, 21; U.S. Marshals Service: Shane T. McCoy, 5, 13, 15, 24–25;
Wikimedia: U.S. Marshals Service, 6, 26

Design Elements by Shutterstock

Printed and bound in the USA.
010757S18

Table of
Contents

The U.S. Marshals Service

You catch a **suspect** on the run and make the arrest. You take him to jail. Then you take a different prisoner to court. You are a U.S. marshal. This is just one day on the job.

suspect—someone who may be responsible for a crime

Just PART of the Job President George Washington began the U.S. Marshals Service in 1789.

U.S. marshals support the **federal** courts. They do this in many ways. They make arrests. They move prisoners. They keep **witnesses** safe.

A U.S. marshal walks a prisoner into a courtroom.

federal—having to do with the national government

witness—a person who has seen or heard a crime

Becoming a U.S. Marshal

Becoming a U.S. marshal is not easy.

Few people who want the job get it.

Marshals must be fit and strong.

They must pass a **background check**.

background check—the process of looking up
and compiling information about a person

Just PART of the Job

U.S. marshals do their training at a school in Glynco, Georgia.

Training is about five months long. Marshals learn about the law and the courts. They learn how to make arrests and how to control prisoners. They go through tough physical training.

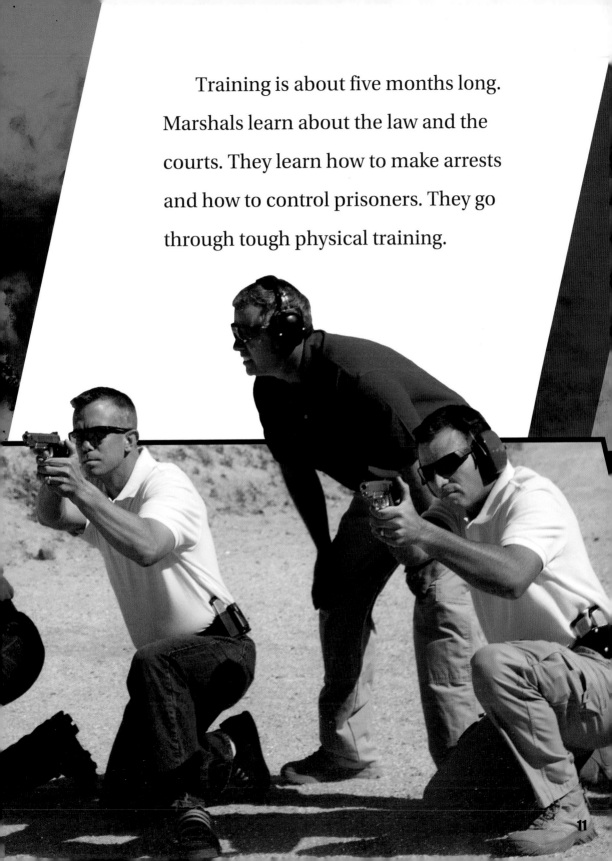

Capture and Transport

Making arrests is a big part of a marshal's job. They arrest people wanted for crimes. They capture **fugitives**. They find people who escaped from jail.

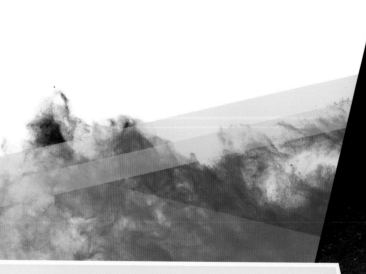

fugitive—a person charged with a crime who runs away from the law

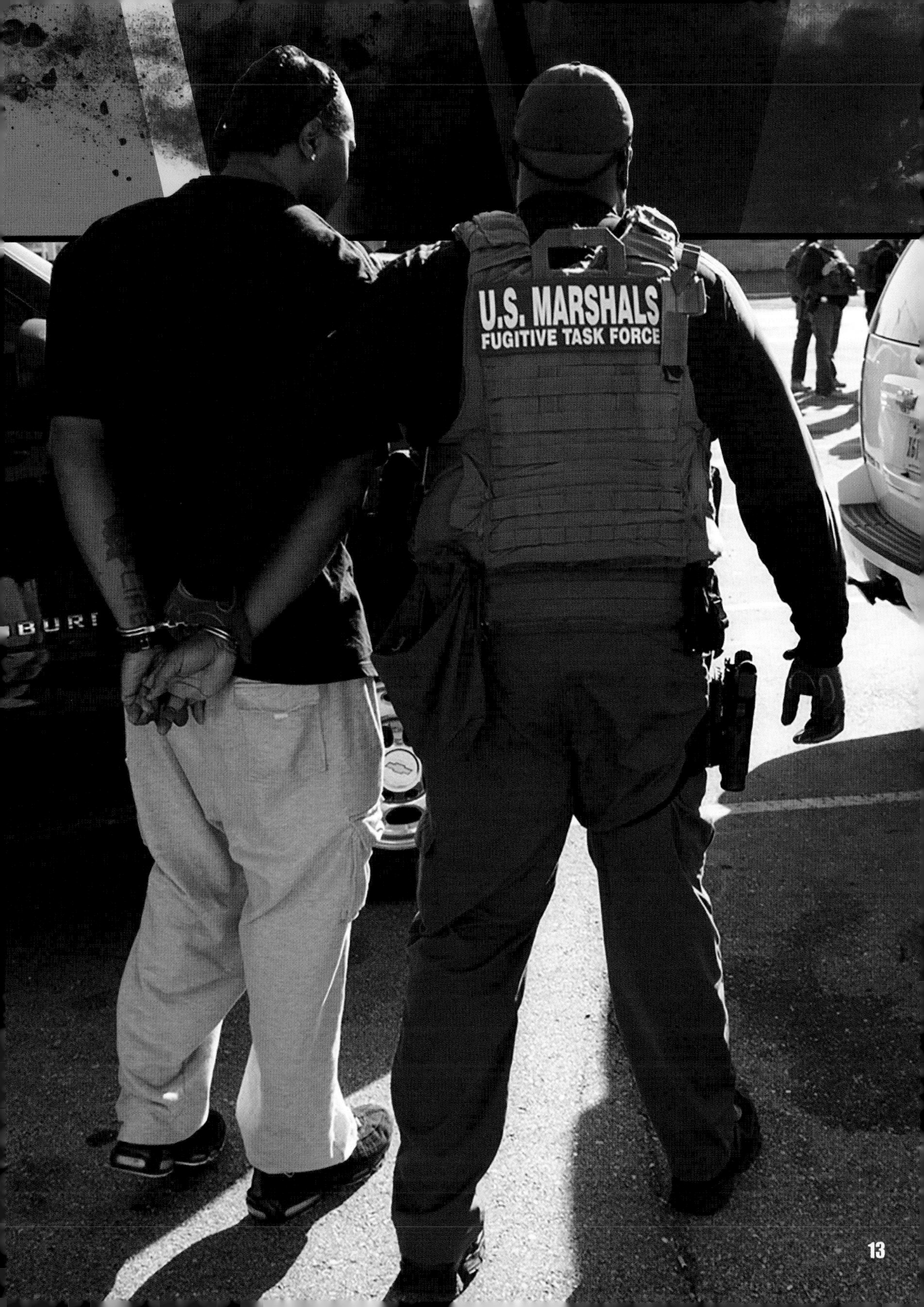
U.S. MARSHALS
FUGITIVE TASK FORCE

Just PART of the Job The U.S. marshals keep a list of their 15 Most Wanted. The most dangerous fugitives are on the list.

Marshals must be ready for anything. They may **raid** a home. They break inside to look for suspects. Suspects may be armed and dangerous. They may try to run and hide. Marshals are ready for the chase.

raid—a sudden, surprise attack on a place

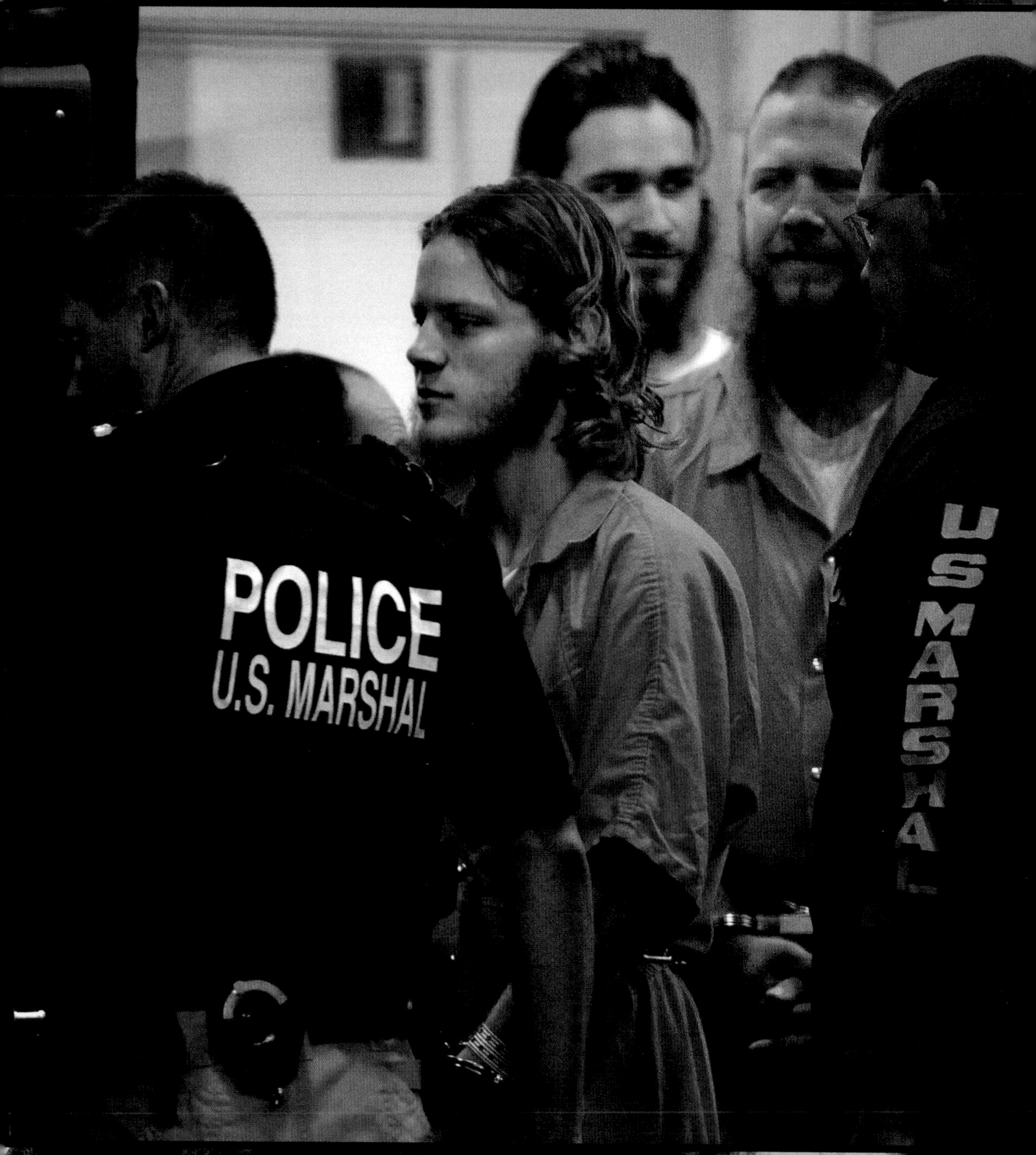
POLICE
U.S. MARSHAL
US MARSHAL

U.S. marshals move prisoners too.
A prisoner might need to go to court.
Marshals drive him or her there.
Some prisoners need to move
from one prison to another.
Marshals take them.

Just PART of the Job
Each day U.S. marshals take more than 2,200 prisoners to court.

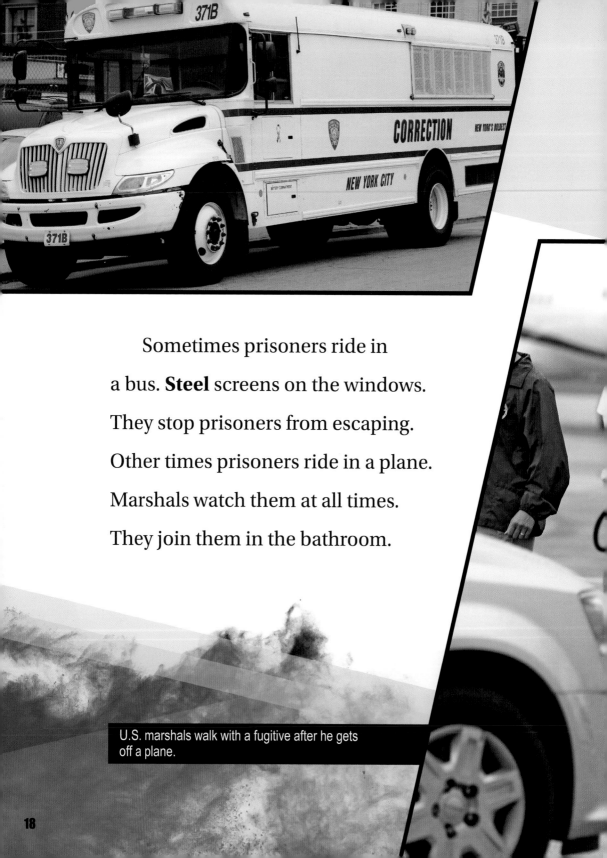

Sometimes prisoners ride in a bus. **Steel** screens on the windows. They stop prisoners from escaping. Other times prisoners ride in a plane. Marshals watch them at all times. They join them in the bathroom.

U.S. marshals walk with a fugitive after he gets off a plane.

Just PART of the Job

Federal air marshals ride on some **commercial** flights. They help keep passengers safe. They are not part of the U.S. Marshals Service.

steel—a hard, strong metal

commercial—to do with business use rather than private use

Protection

Criminals sometimes want to hurt people who **testify** against them. Marshals help keep the witnesses safe. After the trial the witnesses get new names. Marshals help them find new homes and new jobs.

Just PART of the Job

Marshals take belongings from people accused of crimes. They might take homes, cars, and jewelry.

testify—to state facts in court during a trial

There are 400 federal courts in the United States. U.S. marshals help protect these buildings and the workers inside them. They protect the U.S. **Supreme Court** building too. They keep the **justices** safe.

Supreme Court—the most powerful court in the United States

justice—a member of the country's highest court

Types of Marshals

Most marshals are deputies. They may do any job of the U.S. Marshals Service. Deputies work in offices all over the country.

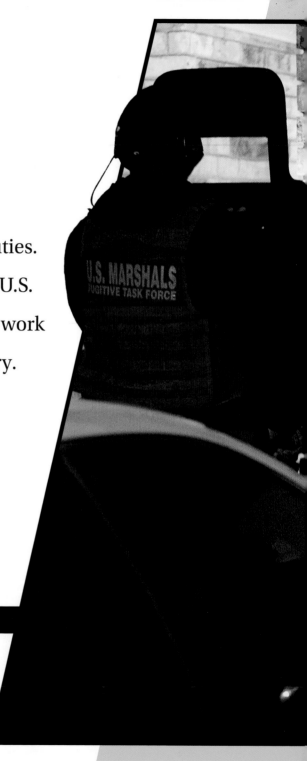

U.S. marshals get ready for a raid.

Some marshals work in **cells**. They **book** prisoners. They search prisoners for weapons and drugs. They take fingerprints.

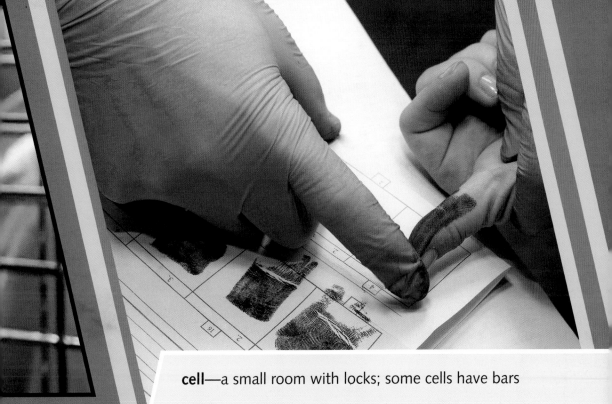

Court security officers work in court buildings. They check each visitor. They make sure no one brings in a weapon. They keep the buildings and people safe.

Just PART of the Job K-9s work for the U.S. Marshals Service. The dogs sniff for bombs and other explosives.

Glossary

background check (BAK-graund CHEK)—the process of looking up and compiling information about a person

book (BUK)—to enter charges against a suspect

cell (SEL)—a small room with locks; some cells have bars

commercial (kuh-MUHR-shuhl)—to do with business use rather than private use

federal (FE-duh-ruhl)—having to do with the national government

fugitive (FYOO-juh-tiv)—a person charged with a crime who runs away from the law

justice (JUHSS-tiss)—a member of the country's highest court

raid (RAYD)—a sudden, surprise attack on a place

steel (STEEL)—a hard, strong metal

Supreme Court (suh-PREEM KORT)—the most powerful court in the United States

suspect (SUH-spekt)—someone who may be responsible for a crime

testify (TESS-tuh-fye)—to state facts in court during a trial

witness (WIT-niss)—a person who has seen or heard a crime

Read More

Cane, Ella. *The U.S. Supreme Court.* Our Government. North Mankato, Minn.: Capstone Press, 2014.

Johnson, Cheri. *Law Enforcement.* Origins: Whodunnit. Fremont, Calif.: Full Tilt Press, 2017.

Rogers, Kate. *Air Marshals.* Careers for Heroes. New York: PowerKids Press, 2016.

Internet Sites

Use FactHound to find Internet sites related to this book.

Visit *www.facthound.com*

Just type in 9781543501407 and go.

Check out projects, games and lots more at **www.capstonekids.com**

Index

DATE DUE			

04/18